Edited by Beverly G. Anu and Nadia Wong-Sang
Cover illustrated by Ha Pham
Inside illustrated by Rachel Carlson

Text Copyright © 2021 by Tiffney T. Laing
Cover and Interior Illustrations Copyright © 2021 by Bevy & Dave, LLC

All rights reserved. No part of this publication may be reproduced, stored in a retrieval system, or transmitted in any form or by any means, electronic, mechanical, photocopying, recorded, or otherwise, without written permission from its publisher. For more information address Bevy & Dave Publishing, P.O. Box 1142, Ashburn, VA 20146.

First Edition

Printed in China

ISBN: 978-1-7374217-0-2

www.bevyanddave.com

DEDICATION

To my ancestors, thank you for your resilience, leadership, and sacrifice.

To my daughter Beverly, being your mom is my greatest gift. Thank you for inspiring me to be my best self.

To the next generation of leaders: may you embrace your rich heritage of leadership, honor your ancestors, be your best selves and create positive change in the world.

This special edition journal was created to support the development of young leaders through reflection, education, and inspiration. It is designed to encourage and motivate the youth to reach their full potential, spark curiosity about Black history, and inspire them to contribute their best to society.

This journal uses the **L.E.G.A.C.Y** Self-Leadership model developed by Tiffney T. Laing in 2009, as a self-guiding tool to be used through the process of becoming your best self. With this journal, children will learn more about themselves, their ancestors, and their great heritage of leadership. Young leaders will be empowered to shape their lives and imagine unlimited possibilities for themselves, their community, and the world.

This Journal Belongs To:

Draw a picture of yourself!

NAME:

_____

AGE:

_____

DATE:

_____

YOUR JOURNEY

INTRODUCTION

APPRECIATION
Chapter 4

COMMITMENT
Chapter 5

SELF-LEADERSHIP
PLEDGE

Carter G. Woodson

1875-1950
Founder of Black History Month
Virginia, United States

INTRODUCTION

YOU MUST GIVE YOUR OWN STORY TO THE WORLD.

Carter G. Woodson

SELF-LEADERSHIP

Hello Friend!

Did you know that you are a leader? I hope so, because it's true, our <u>ancestors'</u> legacy of self-leadership is proof! You see, **self-leadership means to be your best self; to influence yourself to achieve and contribute your best to society.** You have the natural ability to lead because leadership lives in you.

L.E.G.A.C.Y; each letter in the word legacy represents a self-leadership rule. If you follow these six rules you will understand what it means to lead yourself through an incredible life journey, just as our ancestors.

ANCESTOR - Someone born before you who shares your heritage.

LEGACY MODEL

CHAPTER 1

COLOR ME IN!

Rafael Cordero

1790–1868
"Father of Public Education"
in Puerto Rico
San Juan, Puerto Rico

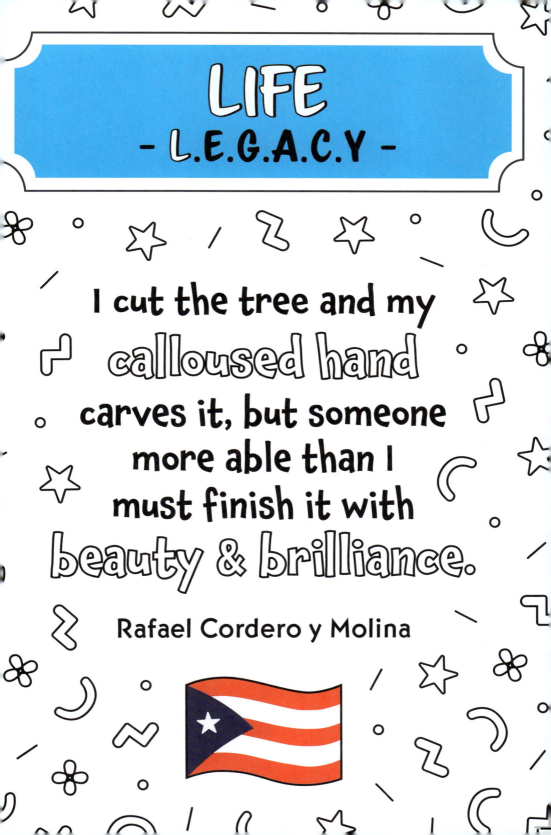

The first rule is **Life.**
You must honor your life by being your best self. How you live your life is your <u>legacy</u> in the making. Your actions, no matter the size, will impact not only your life, but that of your family, community, and society for generations to come because we are all connected.

Being your best self is the ultimate contribution you can make in the world. You must do your part; you never know how you will inspire others. Leadership lives in you!

<u>LEGACY</u> - What you pass down and are remembered by.

I AM A LEADER!
(DOODLE HERE)

OUR HISTORY

Around the globe, our ancestors have shown us the power we have as individuals and as a community to help make the world a better place. By contributing their best to society, regardless of circumstance, our ancestors have inspired generations to be their best selves.

Being your best self takes self-leadership. It requires dedication, becoming aware of who you are, and loving yourself. You truly can achieve whatever you dream because you were born to lead.

LIFE

Black history is a story of leadership that teaches us that no matter what lies in your past, your future awaits you and it begins with first honoring your life. Learn from your ancestors, read their stories, embrace your rich heritage of leadership, and lead yourself through a remarkable life journey.

Every Generation must do their part. Trust yourself, **leadership lives in you!**

WHO ARE YOU?

Your character traits reveal who you are and can help you achieve your dreams.

Circle the traits that best describe you.

Helpful	Kind	Brave
Thoughtful	Hopeful	Optimistic
Trustworthy	Cheerful	Peaceful
Energetic	Brilliant	Friendly
Compassionate	Curious	Funny
Observant	Adventurous	Active
Loving	Respectful	Playful
Strong	Imaginative	Reliable

You can add more character traits below:

_____

_____

_____

_____

LIFE

Add your favorite (7) character traits below:

I am
_____

I am
_____

I am
_____

I am
_____

I am
_____

I am
_____

I am
_____

LIFE

Your actions can create lasting memories for yourself and others.

How can you use your favorite character traits to brighten someone's day?

DISCOVER YOUR ANCESTORS

Lorraine Hansberry Arthur George Gaston • Mae C. Jemison

There is so much to learn from our ancestors. Their experiences and achievements teach us that leadership lives in us. Being connected to your heritage requires curiosity. Keep your ancestors close to your heart, for we have them to thank for the opportunities we enjoy today.

Muhammad Ali • Henry Louis Gates Jr. Patricia Bath

Look at the names around the stars. Discover your ancestors and learn more about them. You can gather information from the library, a bookstore, or the internet.

Choose (1) ancestor and write about them:

⟶

Tererai Trent Valerie L. Thomas

Robert L. Johnson James Baldwin

MY ANCESTOR'S STORY

LIFE

ACHIEVEMENT(S):

_____
_____
_____
_____
_____

NAME:
_____

SOURCE:

_____
_____
_____

AUTHOR:

_____
_____
_____

DAILY MANTRA

I love myself.

I believe in my abilities.

I will honor my life and rich heritage by using my gifts to contribute my best to society.

EXPRESS YOURSELF

What's on your mind and heart?

Date: _____

EXPRESS YOURSELF

What's on your mind and heart?

Date: _____

EXPRESS YOURSELF

What's on your mind and heart?

Date: _____

CHAPTER 2

COLOR ME IN!

Mary McLeod Bethune

1875-1955
Entrepreneur, Educator, Civil and
Women's Rights Leader
South Carolina, United States

The second rule is **Energy.**
<u>Energy</u> is simply your thoughts and actions. Your thoughts are usually followed by actions, which contributes to your experiences. Therefore, *think positive!*

Expect great things to happen, put forth your best effort, have good intentions and treat others the way you want to be treated. Healthy thoughts and actions are seeds to being your best self.

<u>ENERGY</u> - Your thoughts and actions are a source of good or bad energy.

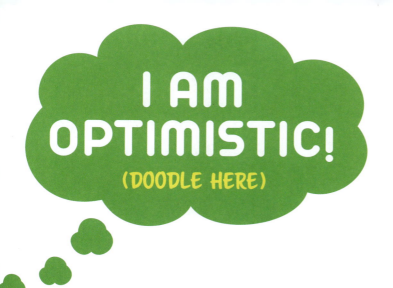

OUR HISTORY

Black history is filled with the spirit of **excellence**. Our ancestors made what seemed impossible, possible by thinking positive and creating solutions to make the world a better place. Our spirit of excellence is found in how we express love through kindness, gratitude, and forgiveness. You can see and feel our excellence in our strength, courage, creativity, determination, and unwavering faith.

ENERGY

Though our ancestors faced many challenges, they were **not victims, but victors.** They were resilient leaders who remained hopeful and became entrepreneurs, inventors, scientists, chemists, historians, engineers, artists, entertainers, athletes, politicians, judges, community organizers, activists, curators, authors, film directors, poets, journalists, astronauts, mathematicians, educators, and more.

Our ancestors contributed their best to society. Their spirit of excellence lives in you.
Leadership lives in you!

> **EXCELLENCE** - *To be outstanding. To do things well and with great care.*
> **VICTOR** - *Winner; someone who overcomes.*

ENERGY

No matter your age,
you can achieve whatever
you set your mind to do.

Name (3) things you hope to do presently or in the future.

1. _____
   _____
   _____

2. _____
   _____
   _____

3. _____
   _____
   _____

DISCOVER YOUR HERITAGE

Reginald Lewis

Bessie V. Blount

Explore and discover our global <u>heritage</u> of leadership. Study our accomplishments and impact around the world. As you learn more, your confidence will grow.

Mansa Musa

Ellen Johnson Sirleaf

Wangari M. Maathai

Philip Emeagwali

HERITAGE - Cultural identity. Values and traditions.

Kamala Harris

Arturo Alfonso Schomburg

Laurent & Larry Bourgeois

Ilia Calderon

Look at the names that are displayed. Discover your ancestors and learn more about them. You can gather information from the library, a bookstore, or the internet.

Choose (1) ancestor and write about them:

ENERGY

MY ANCESTOR'S STORY

ACHIEVEMENT(S):

_____
_____
_____
_____
_____

NAME:
_____

SOURCE:

_____
_____
_____

AUTHOR:

_____
_____
_____

DAILY MANTRA

I love myself.

I believe in my abilities.

I will honor my life and rich heritage by using my gifts to contribute my best to society.

EXPRESS YOURSELF

What's on your mind and heart?

Date: _____

EXPRESS YOURSELF

What's on your mind and heart?

Date: _____

EXPRESS YOURSELF

What's on your mind and heart?

Date: _____

CHAPTER 3

COLOR ME IN!

Les Twins

Laurent and Larry Bourgeois

1988-

Dance Artists

Paris, France

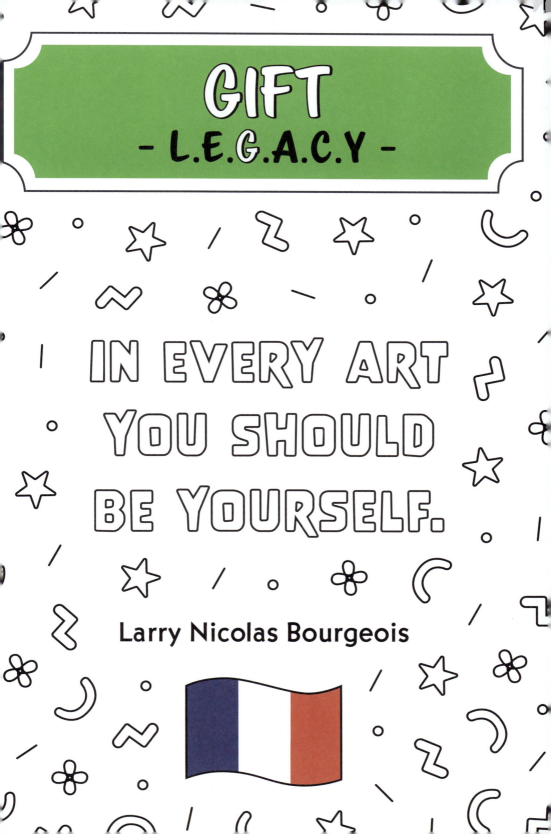

The third rule is **Gift.**
Use your gift(s); your *unique abilities*.
Everyone has a <u>gift</u>. Take time to explore the things you are good at. Imagination can open your gifts' full potential. Imagine a world filled with unlimited possibilities. Be creative and believe. The world needs you.

<u>*GIFT*</u> *- Your natural abilities.*

I AM CREATIVE!

(DOODLE HERE)

OUR HISTORY

Our ancestors have **shaped nations with their gifts, talents, culture, and creativity.** We helped to design Washington, D.C., the Capital of the United States, and enhanced our society by improving the lightbulb, making the widespread use of electric light possible. Our ancestors performed the first successful open-heart surgery, and invented mobile refrigeration, which in turn paved the way for the grocery store industry in the USA.

We helped to save lives by inventing America's first blood bank, the three-way traffic signal, the early gas mask, and railway telegraphy, which made railroad travel safe.

Hip-Hop DJ turntable

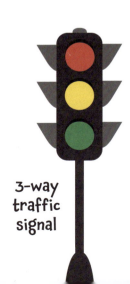

3-way traffic signal

GIFT

gas mask

pioneers of a variety of music genres

Our ancestors built educational and faith-based institutions to educate and uplift our communities. We have established medical centers, financial services, and a host of other businesses representing diverse industries. We have created new forms of artistic expression and have an undeniable global influence on popular culture and trends. We are the pioneers of Blues, Jazz, Rhythm & Blues, Reggae, Hip-Hop, and Gospel music. Our ancestors are beyond remarkable; be proud of your heritage. **Leadership lives in you!**

Washington, DC

Every gift is needed to make the world a better place.

As of today, _____
(DATE)
my gift(s)/talent(s) include:

Example(s): Encouraging people, a good listener
_____
_____
_____
_____

What do you **love most** about your gift(s)?

_____
_____
_____
_____

GIFT

**Imagine using your gift(s).
What are you doing?**

BE CURIOUS!

Augusta Savage

Marie Van Brittan Brown

Shirley Chisholm

Daniel H. Williams

Matthew Henson

Look at the names around the stars.
Discover an ancestor's unique gifts and learn how
they contributed to the betterment of our world.
You can gather information from the library,
a bookstore, or the internet.

Choose (1) ancestor and write about them:
──────────▶

Paul Robeson

Serena & Venus Williams

Emmit J. McHenry

Michelle Obama

John Mack Young

Cicely Tyson

GIFT

MY ANCESTOR'S STORY

NAME:
_____
_____

GIFT(S)/TALENT(S):
_____
_____
_____

HOW DID THEY USE THEIR GIFT(S)/TALENT(S)?
_____
_____
_____
_____

HOW DO THEY INSPIRE YOU?
_____
_____
_____
_____

SOURCE:
_____
_____

AUTHOR:
_____
_____

DAILY MANTRA

I love myself.

I believe in my abilities.

I will honor my life and rich heritage by using my gifts to contribute my best to society.

EXPRESS YOURSELF

What's on your mind and heart?

Date: _____

_____

_____

_____

_____

_____

_____

_____

_____

_____

_____

_____

_____

_____

_____

_____

EXPRESS YOURSELF

What's on your mind and heart?

Date: _____

_____

_____

_____

_____

_____

_____

_____

_____

_____

_____

_____

_____

_____

_____

EXPRESS YOURSELF

What's on your mind and heart?

Date: _____

CHAPTER 4

COLOR ME IN!

Oprah Winfrey

1954–
Entrepreneur, Talk Show Host,
Actress and Philanthropist
Mississippi, United States

NO GESTURE IS TOO SMALL WHEN DONE WITH GRATITUDE.

Oprah Winfrey

The fourth rule is Appreciation.

Demonstrate your gratitude not only through words, but with your actions. Saying "thank you" is one way to express your appreciation, but it is felt much deeper when shared through acts of kindness.

Being your best self and contributing your best to society shows appreciation for your life and others.

APPRECIATION - Recognition of the good in someone or something.

GRATITUDE - An expression of your appreciation.

I AM GRATEFUL!

(DOODLE HERE)

OUR HISTORY

Our history reveals the power of appreciation. Through the ups and downs our ancestors were grateful for the opportunity to live, to be, to do. They were eager to secure a better future for their *descendants* (you).

Their actions teach us that **it is our responsibility to show our appreciation through acts of service.** Our ancestors teach us that life is what we make it and that we are to be grateful for opportunities to love, to learn, to give, to encourage, and to be our best selves. We have much to be grateful for and many to thank.

APPRECIATION

Learn from our ancestors, express your appreciation not just through your words, but through your actions. Your <u>service</u> in this world will reveal who you are. Be your best self, **leadership lives in you!**

DESCENDANT – The offspring of previous generations.

SERVICE – To be helpful.

ENCOURAGE

ACTS OF SERVICE TRAIN

EXPRESS YOUR APPRECIATION

Expressing gratitude to those around you is an important act of service for you and encouraging for the recipient. Write a note of appreciation to someone in your family that you want to recognize for their **service.** Next, hand deliver it or send it through the postal service.

Write your draft below:

DRAFT

Date: _____

Dear _____,

_____

_____

_____

_____

_____

_____

_____

_____

APPRECIATION

EVERYDAY HEROES

All around you are people contributing to the betterment of our world. However, many acts of service go unrecognized. Discover a local community leader today. For example, an educator, coach, historian, volunteer, activist, etc.

Write a note of appreciation to someone you want to recognize for their service. Next, send it through e-mail or the postal service. **Write your draft below:**

NOTE OF APPRECIATION

DRAFT

Dear _____,

DAILY MANTRA

I love myself.

I believe in my abilities.

I will honor my life and rich heritage by using my gifts to contribute my best to society.

EXPRESS YOURSELF

What's on your mind and heart?

Date: _____

EXPRESS YOURSELF

What's on your mind and heart?

Date: _____

EXPRESS YOURSELF

What's on your mind and heart?

Date: _____

CHAPTER 5

COLOR ME IN!

Nelson Mandela

1918-2013
Activist, Former President of South Africa
Mvezo, South Africa

COMMITMENT
- L.E.G.A.C.Y -

IT ALWAYS SEEMS IMPOSSIBLE UNTIL IT'S DONE.

Nelson Mandela

The fifth rule is **Commitment.** <u>Commitment</u> is and will always be the key to accomplishing anything. Whatever you want to do, do it with all of your might. **Never give up** because you were born to lead. Your commitment matters because it impacts not just you, but others too. The world needs you.

<u>COMMITMENT</u> - *To stick to your task and not give up.*

NEVER GIVE UP!

(DOODLE HERE)

OUR HISTORY

Throughout history, our ancestors have shown us the power of commitment. With love and determination on our side, **no challenge has been too difficult to keep us from being our best selves.**

Our unwavering commitment to making the world a better place has influenced nations to enact change. Laws have been created to help communities, programs have been developed to enrich lives, businesses have been established to better serve the needs of people and so much more.

Our heritage of leadership has and will continue to make an impact across the globe. Our ancestors have inspired generations to achieve their dreams. Now it's your turn. **Leadership lives in you!**

COMMITMENT

Name (1) thing you do daily or weekly.

_____
_____
_____

Why are you committed to this activity?

_____
_____
_____

How does this daily activity help you and/or others?

_____
_____
_____

Write a song that will encourage you to never quit. Sing or rap your song whenever you need a reminder that you can achieve your dream.

TIPS FOR WRITING A SONG:

♪ BEGIN WITH A TITLE (THE FOCUS OF YOUR SONG).

♪ CREATE THE SONG'S CHORUS (THE MAIN IDEA OF THE SONG THAT IS REPEATED).

♪ WRITE WORDS THAT RHYME TO CREATE LYRICS.

♪ DEVELOP A MELODY FOR YOUR SONG.

♪ SING/RAP AND REPEAT!

COMMITMENT

MY SONG

Title: _____

_____

_____

_____

_____

_____

_____

_____

_____

_____

Written by: _____

EXPLORE YOUR ROOTS

Look at the names around the road. Discover (1) ancestor who inspires you to never quit. You can gather information from the library, a bookstore, or the internet.

Granville T. Woods

Bessie Coleman

Percy L. Julian

Alice H. Parker

Neil deGrasse Tyson

Maggie L. Walker

Cathy Hughes

Barack Obama

Sheila C. Johnson

Robert Smalls

Shelton Jackson "Spike" Lee

COMMITMENT

MY ANCESTOR'S STORY

THIS ANCESTOR INSPIRES ME BECAUSE:

_____
_____
_____
_____
_____

NAME:
_____

SOURCE:

_____
_____
_____

AUTHOR:

_____
_____
_____

DAILY MANTRA

I love myself.

I believe in my abilities.

I will honor my life and rich heritage by using my gifts to contribute my best to society.

EXPRESS YOURSELF

What's on your mind and heart?

Date: _____

EXPRESS YOURSELF

What's on your mind and heart?

Date: _____

EXPRESS YOURSELF

What's on your mind and heart?

Date: _____

_____
_____
_____
_____
_____
_____
_____
_____
_____
_____
_____
_____
_____
_____
_____

CHAPTER 6

COLOR ME IN!

Marcus Garvey

1887-1940
Entrepreneur, Orator, and Activist
Saint Ann's Bay, Jamaica

YOU
- L.E.G.A.C.Y -

If you have no **confidence** in self, you are twice **defeated** in the race of **life.**

Marcus Garvey

YOU ARE A LEADER!

The sixth and most important rule is **you.** It's all up to you! Leadership begins and ends with you. It is your responsibility to make this world great. Do not look to others to do what you can do.

> **BELIEVE IN YOURSELF; BELIEVE IN YOUR ABILITIES!**

Leadership lives in me!

(DOODLE HERE)

OUR FUTURE

You are extraordinary! You come from a powerful heritage of leadership that lives in you. There is nothing you cannot do. Your ancestors have paved the way for you to achieve and become all that you hope to be. Remember, **you were born to lead**, so lead yourself to victory.

Your actions will inspire others to do their part and together our collective efforts will make our community and the world a better place. Throughout your life journey, keep a positive attitude, believe in your abilities, appreciate life, and commit to being your best self. You are our future; do not fear, for **you are extraordinary. Leadership lives in you.**

YOU

ENCOURAGE YOURSELF

Write yourself a kind note and place it somewhere you can see it every day. **Write your draft below:**

DRAFT

Date: _____

Dear Me,

_____
_____
_____
_____
_____
_____
_____
_____
_____
_____

ENCOURAGE SOMEONE

Words of <u>encouragement</u> can create a beautiful experience and memory for both the recipient and the giver. Write an encouraging note for someone and send it to them through e-mail, the postal service or hand deliver it. **Write your draft below:**

DRAFT

Date: _____

Dear _____ ,

ENCOURAGEMENT - *The act of supporting someone.*

YOU

POEMS FOR YOU

LIFE IS WHAT YOU MAKE IT

As I look around at this great big world,
I wonder what life could bring.
My family said that life is what I make it,
so I know it starts with me.
With all the lives that came before me
with their inspirational stories,
I am confident I can achieve
whatever I dream, because my ancestors'
legacy of leadership lives in me.

- Tiffney T. Laing

YOU ARE A FORCE OF POSITIVE ENERGY

Whether the brightness of the sun or gloom from the cloudy sky surrounds me, I am going to use my mind, spirit, and body to create the day I want it to be. I am a force of positive energy with leadership in me.

— Tiffney T. Laing

YOU

BELIEVE IN THE POSSIBILITIES!

No matter what lies in my past,
a bright future awaits me, and it
begins with first honoring me.
I must know who I am and dare to
achieve what I think of and believe.
My life is filled with possibilities.
Yes! Leadership lives in me.

– Tiffney T. Laing

DAILY MANTRA

I love myself.

I believe in my abilities.

I will honor my life and rich heritage by using my gifts to contribute my best to society.

EXPRESS YOURSELF

What's on your mind and heart?

Date: _____

EXPRESS YOURSELF

What's on your mind and heart?

Date: _____

EXPRESS YOURSELF

What's on your mind and heart?

Date: _____

LETTER FROM THE FOUNDER

Dear Leader,

Congratulations on the completion of your journal! On the following page I have included a self-leadership pledge certificate. Take the pledge as a reminder that you are a leader with unlimited possibilities.

Remember that life is a journey filled with many experiences to help you become your best self. Through your journey, keep love at the center of your existence. You must always love yourself, believe in your abilities, and the possibilities.

With love there are no limits to what you can achieve; it guides you like a compass, pointing you in the right direction towards joy and peace.

I hope this journal inspires you throughout your life. May you be empowered to contribute your best to society, just as your amazing ancestors.

Wishing you love, joy, and courage,
Tiffney T. Laing

SELF-LEADERSHIP PLEDGE

On this day, _____,

I, _____,

pledge to: use leadership in my own life and contribute my best to society.

INSPIRING LEADERSHIP AND DISCOVERY

Established in 2015, Bevy & Dave is an award-winning educational toy company devoted to making the world a better place by changing the narrative of Black history and building leaders.

Our learning tools are created with love and designed to educate, inspire, and empower children to be their best selves.

Learn more about Bevy & Dave at:
www.bevyanddave.com.

Special Thanks:
To my family, friends, and you for supporting Bevy & Dave. I am forever grateful.

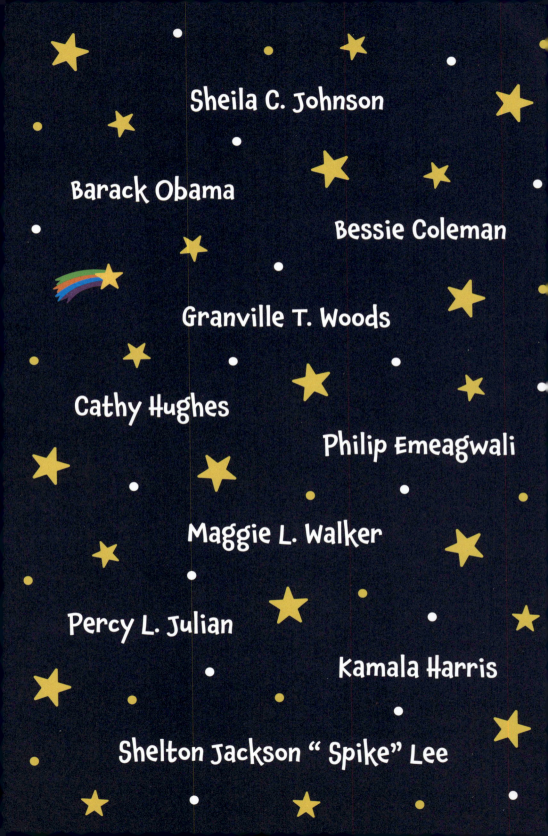

MEET SIMONE BILES

SAM LASKARIS

Lerner Publications ◆ Minneapolis

Free Database Trial: lernersports.com

Love to wife, Kathryn, and sons, Michael and Adam—thanks for lifelong support and encouragement to continue my love of writing.

Copyright © 2025 by Lerner Publishing Group, Inc.

All rights reserved. International copyright secured. No part of this book may be reproduced, stored in a retrieval system, or transmitted in any form or by any means—electronic, mechanical, photocopying, recording, or otherwise—without the prior written permission of Lerner Publishing Group, Inc., except for the inclusion of brief quotations in an acknowledged review.

Lerner Publications Company
An imprint of Lerner Publishing Group, Inc.
241 First Avenue North
Minneapolis, MN 55401 USA

For reading levels and more information, look up this title at www.lernerbooks.com.

Main body text set in Aptifer Slab LT Pro. Typeface provided by Linotype AG.

Editor: Nicole Berglund **Designer:** Martha Kranes

Library of Congress Cataloging-in-Publication Data

Names: Laskaris, Sam, author.
Title: Meet Simone Biles : gymnastics superstar / Sam Laskaris.
Description: Minneapolis, MN : Lerner Publications, [2025] | Series: Lerner sports. Sports VIPs | Includes bibliographical references and index. | Audience: Ages 7–11 | Audience: Grades 2–3 |
Summary: "US gymnastics legend Simone Biles has earned seven Olympic medals and even has five moves named after her! Gymnastics fans will be ecstatic to flip into the life and career of this gymnast"— Provided by publisher.
Identifiers: LCCN 2023052602 (print) | LCCN 2023052603 (ebook) | ISBN 9798765625996 (library binding) | ISBN 9798765629734 (paperback) | ISBN 9798765637609 (epub)
Subjects: LCSH: Biles, Simone 1997-—Juvenile literature. | Women gymnasts—Biography—Juvenile literature. | Olympic athletes—United States—Biography—Juvenile literature.
Classification: LCC GV460.2.B55 L37 2025 (print) | LCC GV460.2.B55 (ebook) | DDC 796.44092 [B]—dc23/eng/20231120

LC record available at https://lccn.loc.gov/2023052602
LC ebook record available at https://lccn.loc.gov/2023052603

Manufactured in the United States of America
1-1010133-51933-2/14/2024

TABLE OF CONTENTS
>>>>>>>>>>>>>>>>

BACK ON THE BEAM	**4**
FAST FACTS	**5**
CHAPTER 1 **CHILDHOOD**	**8**
CHAPTER 2 **GETTING SERIOUS**	**12**
CHAPTER 3 **THE GOAT**	**18**
CHAPTER 4 **LOOKING AHEAD**	**23**
SIMONE BILES CAREER STATS	28
GLOSSARY	29
SOURCE NOTES	30
LEARN MORE	31
INDEX	32

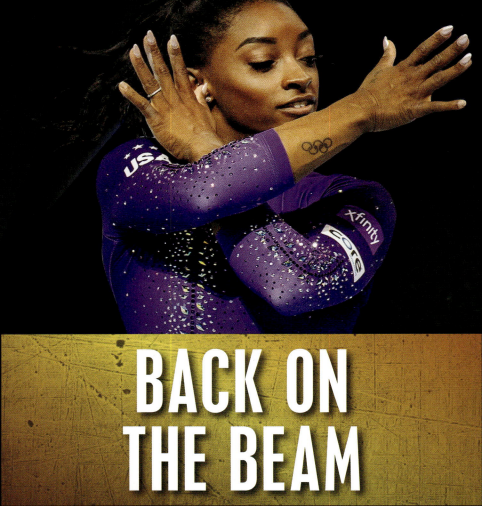

BACK ON THE BEAM

At the 2023 World Championships in Belgium, US gymnast Simone Biles began her balance beam routine with a jump. Once she was on the 4-inch-wide (10 cm) beam, Biles flew into a backward leap. Then she danced low and slow, and spun three times from a crouch. Rising back to her feet, Biles soared across the beam with a series of flips. The routine ended with an amazing dismount. She did it! She won the gold.

It had been two years since Biles had competed in a major meet. She had placed her career on hold after the Tokyo Olympics in 2021. She took time off to focus on her mental health.

FAST FACTS

DATE OF BIRTH: March 14, 1997

TEAM: USA Gymnastics

PROFESSIONAL HIGHLIGHTS: has won 37 total medals from world championships and Olympic Games; has five gymnastics moves named after her; has written a book

PERSONAL HIGHLIGHTS: is an advocate for social issues; received the Presidential Medal of Freedom in 2022; is nicknamed the GOAT

Biles performs on the beam at the 2023 World Championships.

Biles proved she is still a force in gymnastics by winning four gold medals in Belgium. She took top honors for her beam, floor, all-around, and team routines. Biles added a silver medal for her vault.

"I wasn't too worried about medal count or medal color this meet," Biles said in Belgium. "As long as I get out there and do those routines again, it's a win in my book." Biles has won a lot of medals at world meets and the Olympic Games. She has 37 medals, and 27 of them are gold!

In 2016, Biles competed in Rio de Janeiro, Brazil, in her first Olympic Games. Since then, she has dazzled the world with her skills and earned many more medals. But it hasn't been easy. Biles had to work hard to become a champion gymnast.

Biles and her coach celebrate after her all-around gold medal win in Belgium.

CHAPTER 1

CHILDHOOD

Simone Biles was born on March 14, 1997, in Columbus, Ohio. She has an older brother, Tevin; an older sister, Ashley; and a younger sister, Adria (*above*). Their parents couldn't care for them, so the children lived together in a foster home.

When she was six, Simone and her sister Adria were adopted by their grandparents, Ron and Nellie Biles. Simone's other two siblings were adopted by their aunt in Ohio. Simone grew up in Spring, within Houston, Texas. Although that was far from Columbus, Simone was very happy when her grandparents became her mom and dad. "[They] support me in any way possible," Biles said.

Simone attends a Houston Astros baseball game with her parents, Ron and Nellie Biles, in 2016.

Biles grew up in Spring, Texas, within the Houston area.

Simone enjoyed being in Texas for another reason. Her parents had a trampoline. She was able to bounce and flip on it as much as she wanted. She had lots of energy and enjoyed doing tricks.

Soon after moving to Texas, Simone went on a field trip to a gym. A coach noticed Simone's energy and thought she might do well as a gymnast. The coach asked Simone's parents to put her in classes.

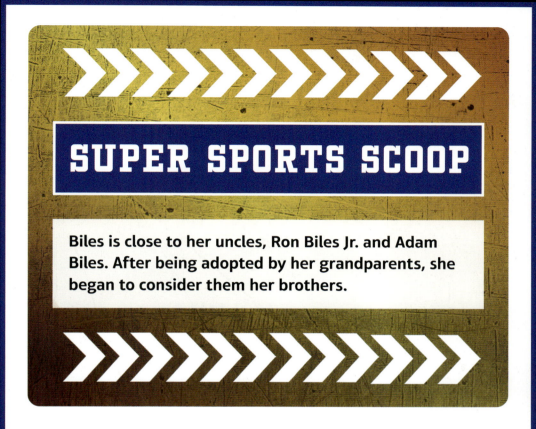

SUPER SPORTS SCOOP

Biles is close to her uncles, Ron Biles Jr. and Adam Biles. After being adopted by her grandparents, she began to consider them her brothers.

Simone joined Bannon's Gymnastix in Houston when she was six. She had fun doing jumps and backflips. Before long, she could perform as well as the older gymnasts. And people took notice.

CHAPTER 2

GETTING SERIOUS

Simone was a natural at gymnastics. She made it look easy. Women's gymnastics has four events: floor exercise, balance beam, uneven bars, and vault. She could flip and turn on a narrow balance beam and dance her way through a floor routine. Flipping above the vault was a breeze, as was swinging between the uneven bars.

Simone quickly moved through the classes at Bannon's Gymnastix. Her coaches helped her improve her skills and win at competitions. When she was 13, she won her first two medals at the US Women's Junior Olympic National Championships. After that, she took part in elite competitions.

Biles (*top*) warms up with her teammates at Bannon's Gymnastix in 2013.

Simone continued to win at her sport. But practice took up a lot of her time. She left public school when she was 14 and took classes at home. This allowed her to practice more and improve her skills. She stood out from other gymnasts with the difficult moves she performed in her routines.

In 2012, Simone joined the US Women's Junior National Team. The following year, she advanced to the senior team. Gymnasts who are picked for national teams travel to different meets around the world. They can improve their skills and compete with gymnasts from other countries.

Biles wins the all-around gold medal at the 2012 Secret US Classic.

Biles performs on the vault at the 2013 US National Championships.

At her first world competition in 2013, Simone won the all-around gold medal. "None of it seemed real," she said of her world title. "People ask me now, 'What was going through your head as you went up to the podium?' and all I can remember thinking is, *Did this just happen*?"

This was the first highlight for Simone on the world stage. Many more were yet to come.

Biles performs on the beam in 2013.

Biles poses for a photo with her competitors after winning the all-around gold at the 2013 US National Championships.

SUPER SPORTS SCOOP

Biles has two French bulldogs, Lilo and Rambo. She enjoys sharing pictures of them on Instagram. The dogs have 75,000 followers, while Biles has seven million!

CHAPTER 3

THE GOAT

Simone Biles is no one-hit wonder. She has competed in six world championships since 2013, and 2023 marked her sixth all-around world championship win. She has won 30 world medals, including 23 gold. This means she has more world medals than any other gymnast in history! Fans like to call her the GOAT, or greatest of all time.

On top of her world championship wins, Biles also competed in the 2016 and 2021 Olympic Games. In the 2016 games in Brazil, Biles proved herself to the world with gold medals in the individual all-around, vault, and floor exercise. She also earned a bronze medal on the balance beam and a gold medal in the team event. Many people compared her to other Olympic greats. "I'm not the next Usain Bolt or Michael Phelps. I'm the first Simone Biles," she said in 2016.

Biles leaps during her floor routine at the 2016 Olympic Games.

Biles performs on the balance beam at the 2021 Olympic Games.

The 4 feet 8 (1.4 m) star continued to set herself apart at the 2021 Olympics in Japan. After winning one bronze and one silver medal, Biles withdrew from the competition to focus on her mental health. She later shared that she had the twisties. That is when a gymnast loses track of where they are while twisting in the air. The twisties can lead to a serious injury. That's especially true for an athlete like Biles, who performs hard moves.

Biles soars over the balance beam during her routine at the Olympic Games in Japan.

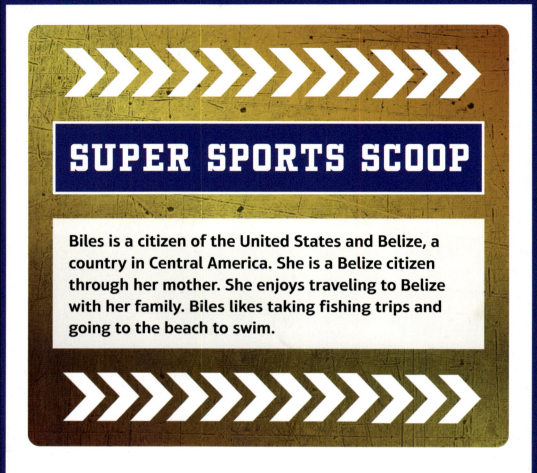

SUPER SPORTS SCOOP

Biles is a citizen of the United States and Belize, a country in Central America. She is a Belize citizen through her mother. She enjoys traveling to Belize with her family. Biles likes taking fishing trips and going to the beach to swim.

Most fans supported Biles's decision to withdraw, but others criticized her. They thought she should have competed for her country. People thought that by leaving the competition, she was a quitter. But Biles knew what was best for her and her health. Competing with the twisties is dangerous.

CHAPTER 4

LOOKING AHEAD

In July 2022, Simone Biles got another important medal. She received the Presidential Medal of Freedom from US president Joe Biden. The medal is one of the highest honors awarded to citizens by the US government. She received the medal for her work away from the gym. Biles has used her fame to speak about mental health, improving the US foster care system, and more.

Biles wanted to bring awareness to mental health issues in sports. "I don't think [people] take into consideration [athletes'] mental health," she said. "We're not just athletes or entertainment. We're human too and we have emotions and feelings. . . . I just think it's something that people should be more aware of."

Biles speaks at an event in California in 2022.

Biles performs on the balance beam at a competition in 2023.

Some fans thought that 2021 was the end of Biles's career as a gymnast. They wondered if the star would ever return to her sport. But in 2023, she made an exciting comeback. Biles won big at the US Classic in Illinois, clinching the all-around title along with a bronze medal on the uneven bars, and two gold medals for her balance

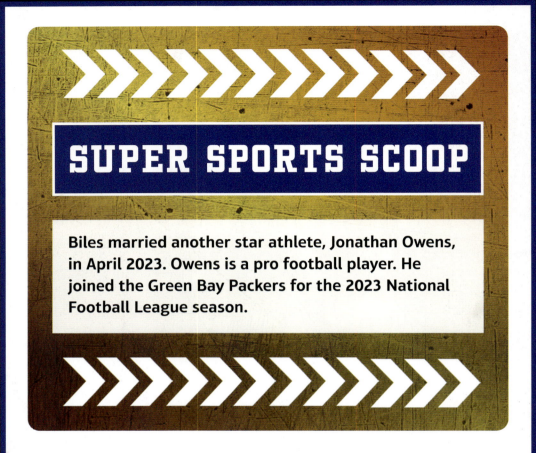

SUPER SPORTS SCOOP

Biles married another star athlete, Jonathan Owens, in April 2023. Owens is a pro football player. He joined the Green Bay Packers for the 2023 National Football League season.

beam and floor exercise. Then she won again with the all-around title at a selection camp in Texas. That meet decided which athletes would be on the US team at the world championships in Belgium.

Biles dominated at the World Championships. She won four gold medals and a silver. Despite her two-year break, she was as talented as ever. She continued to train with the hope of competing in the Olympics in 2024. Fans can't wait to see what she does next!

Biles flips during her performance at the 2023 World Championships.

SIMONE BILES CAREER STATS

OLYMPIC GOLD MEDALS:

4

WORLD CHAMPIONSHIP GOLD MEDALS:

23

OLYMPIC SILVER MEDALS:

1

WORLD CHAMPIONSHIP SILVER MEDALS:

4

OLYMPIC BRONZE MEDALS:

2

WORLD CHAMPIONSHIP BRONZE MEDALS:

3

Stats are accurate through December 2023.

GLOSSARY

all-around: when a gymnast competes in all events and is given a score in each event

balance beam: an event in which gymnasts compete on a 4-inch-wide (10 cm) beam

elite: the top level in a sport

floor exercise: an event in which gymnasts perform dance steps and tumbling moves on a 40-square-foot (3.7 sq. m) mat

meet: a gymnastics competition that includes different events

routine: the series of moves that gymnasts perform

team event: when a gymnastics team competes in all the events and is given a score in each

twisties: when a gymnast loses track of where they are in the air

uneven bars: an event in which gymnasts compete on two bars at different heights

vault: an event in which gymnasts launch from a springboard to a vaulting table and then into the air

SOURCE NOTES

6   Nancy Armour, "Simone Biles Finishes with Four Golds at 2023 Gymnastics World Championships," *USA Today*, October 8, 2023, https://www.usatoday.com/story/sports/olympics/2023/10/08/simone-biles-at-2023-gymnastics-world-championships-live-updates/71099947007/.

9   Julie Tremaine, "All about Simone Biles' Parents, Ronald and Nellie Biles," *People*, August 7, 2023, https://people.com/sports/all-about-ronald-nellie-biles-simone-biles-parents/.

16 Simone Biles, *Courage to Soar: A Body in Motion, a Life in Balance* (Grand Rapids, MI: Zondervan, 2016), 169.

19 Kristina Rodulfo, "Simone Biles Would Like You to Not Compare Her to Male Athletes," *Elle*, August 11, 2016, https://www.elle.com/culture/news/a38468/simone-biles-im-not-the-next-usain-bolt-michael-phelps/.

24 Jacob Camenker, "Simone Biles Opens Up about Mental Health: 'We're Not Just Athletes or Entertainment. We're Human Too,'" *Sporting News*, August 4, 2021, https://www.sportingnews.com/us/athletics/news/simone-biles-mental-health-athletes/2wda61k16m84zzjgam0iz7ye.

LEARN MORE

Anderson, Josh. *Simone Biles vs. Nadia Comaneci: Who Would Win?* Minneapolis: Lerner Publications, 2024.

Kiddle: Gymnastics Facts for Kids
https://kids.kiddle.co/Gymnastics

Nnachi, Ngeri. *Raising the Bar: Black Women Who Changed Gymnastics.* Minneapolis: Lerner Publications, 2025.

Olympics: Simone Biles
https://olympics.com/en/athletes/simone-biles

Sabelko, Rebecca. *Simone Biles.* Minneapolis: Bellwether Media, 2023.

Simone Biles
https://simonebiles.com

INDEX

all-around, 6, 16, 18–19, 25–26

balance beam, 4–6, 12, 19, 25–26
Bannon's Gymnastix, 11, 13

floor exercise, 6, 12, 19, 26

Houston, Texas, 9, 11

Olympic Games, 5, 7, 13, 19, 21, 26

twisties, 21–22

uneven bars, 12, 25
US Women's Junior National Team, 14
US Women's Senior National Team, 14

vault, 6, 12, 19

World Championships, 4–6, 16, 18–19, 26

PHOTO ACKNOWLEDGMENTS

Images: Tim Clayton/Corbis/Getty Images, p.4; AP Photo/DIRK WAEM/Belga/Sipa USA, p. 6; AP Photo/Virginia Mayo, p. 7; Smiley N. Pool/Houston Chronicle/Getty Images, pp. 8, 12, 13; Melissa Phillip/Houston Chronicle/Getty Images, p. 9; Silvio Ligutti/Shutterstock, p. 10; ZUMA Press, Inc./Alamy, p. 14; AP Photo/Elise Amendola, pp. 15, 17; Tim Clayton/Corbis/Getty Images, p. 16; AP Photo/© Amy Sanderson/ZUMA Wire, p. 18; AP Photo/Rebecca Blackwell, p. 19; AP Photo/Kyodo, p. 20; Laurence Griffiths/Getty Images, p. 21; AP Photo/Susan Walsh, p. 23; Alberto E. Rodriguez/Getty Images, p. 24; Stacy Revere/Getty Images, p. 25; Tim Clayton/Corbis/Getty Images, p. 27.

Cover: Andre Paes/Alamy.